I REMEMBER…
MY POP CULTURE

100 memorable pop culture moments
1924 - 1984

I REMEMBER...
MY POP CULTURE

100 memorable pop culture moments
1924 - 1984

R. H. PAULSON

"Everybody needs his memories. They keep the wolf of insignificance from the door."
—Saul Bellow

To Mom and Dad:
Thanks for the memories

TABLE OF CONTENTS

INTRODUCTION

Eighty-five-year-old Sophie's eyes sparkled and she began to giggle. I was presenting some of the material in this book to the residents of an assisted living facility. Count Basie's photo had just flashed onto the screen, and Sophie became excited. She told us that six decades earlier she had been a nightclub singer in Washington, DC. Count Basie was in town for a show and recognized her on the street the next day. He offered Sophie's small group of friends a ride. "He was a perfect gentleman," she said. What was most remarkable about Sophie's excitement and her story was that Sophie has experienced some memory loss. But, the photo of Count Basie brought a flood of memories and emotions.

I have been working with the elderly for years throughout the Washington, DC area. As a way to connect with these wonderful people – including those experiencing some memory loss – I began compiling pop culture moments they would remember. Much of that material made its way into this book, which covers the years 1924 - 1984. These six decades are generally the most familiar to both the elderly and their adult baby boomer children. It is fascinating when multiple generations share conversations, songs, stories, movie quotes, and warm feelings. Memories have the power to bring people together because, while a memory is indeed a picture or a thought, it is also an emotion.

I have heard so many stories like Sophie's: the lawyer who once received a phone call from Orson Welles, a Syracuse alumnus reminiscing about Louis Armstrong's gig at his senior dance, and the grand dame who bragged to me about her Hula-Hoop prowess. Remembrances get people talking because a memory rarely travels alone. It's usually accompanied by other memories.

At the time of this writing, both of my parents are in their late seventies. On a recent trip home, I read selections from an early version of this book. It was an afternoon I will never forget. Mom and Dad told me the most amazing stories about the events featured in this collection and how the memories fit into their own lives. I have continued my experiment by talking about these pop culture moments at family reunions, on vacations, and at holiday gatherings. No one seems to tire of sharing their stories.

We baby boomers have our own fond remembrances from the fifties, sixties, seventies, and eighties. Remember *Gilligan's Island*? I can still recall a night, about forty years ago, when a friend slept over at my house and we stayed up late into the night recounting every *Gilligan's Island* episode we could remember.

It's also exciting to share these stories with our children. With TV Land, Turner Classic Movies, new movies such as *Saving Mr. Banks,* and other cultural references, our children are already familiar with many of the people and events in this book. Add your own recollections and stories, and you have a wonderful opportunity to build bridges.

And while the events that I have chosen are just some of the wonderful pop culture moments from these years, this is a collection of memories that will bring generations together. Whether you share its contents with others, or simply read for yourself and rekindle your own fond memories, I hope you enjoy walking down memory lane.

R. H. Paulson

June 2014

1924

First radio broadcast of *National Barn Dance*

During the Roaring Twenties, millions of Americans moved from the countryside to the cities. And rural folks were beginning to connect with the rest of the world via the miracle of radio. Broadcast every Saturday night from Chicago's WLS, *National Barn Dance* was a country variety show similar to the later TV show *Hee Haw*. It featured folk songs, friendly guests, and homespun humor. With an eventual national audience on the NBC Blue Network, the radio show reminded the new city residents of home and celebrated an idealized country culture that rural listeners enjoyed. Millions of Americans could be proud of their rural heritage.

Something you might remember... Guests included the Hoosier Hot Shots, Gene Autry, Eddie Dean, Patsy Montana and the Prairie Ramblers, Lulu Belle, the DeZurik Sisters, and Captain Stubby and the Buccaneers.

Something new to remember... Before his solo career, famous crooner Andy Williams appeared on the show as part of the Williams Brothers.

1925

First radio broadcast of the *Grand Ole Opry*

The show debuted as the *WSM Barn Dance*, broadcast from Nashville, Tennessee. Thirty-year-old George D. Hay, who had started the *National Barn Dance* in Chicago, declared himself the "Solemn Old Judge" and launched the new show on November 28, 1925. That first show featured fiddler "Uncle" Jimmy Thompson, who reportedly claimed he could "fiddle the bugs off a tater vine." One night in 1927, Hay opened the show by joking that the station's previous show, just concluded, had featured music from grand opera but now it was time for "the grand ole opry." The name stuck and has been used ever since.

Something you might remember... Country music legends Hank Williams, Patsy Cline, Roy Acuff, Bill Monroe, and Minnie Pearl (pictured) were show regulars.

Something new to remember... Both Elvis and the Byrds later appeared at the Grand Ole Opry but received cool receptions and were not invited to return.

1925

F. Scott Fitzgerald publishes *The Great Gatsby*

Initially panned by reviewers as "F. Scott Fitzgerald's latest dud," most now agree with T. S. Elliot's prescient view that this is one of the greatest American novels. Inspired by the Long Island North Shore parties Fitzgerald attended in the early 1920s, the book captures the spirit of the great "Jazz Age" (the term Fitzgerald himself invented).

Something you might remember... Key characters include narrator Nick Carraway, Jay Gatsby, Daisy Buchanan, Tom Buchanan, Jordan Baker, and Myrtle Wilson.

Something new to remember... The title page poem is credited to Thomas Parke D'Invilliers—who isn't real. D'Invilliers is a character from Fitzgerald's *This Side of Paradise*.

> Then wear the gold hat, if that will move her;
> If you can bounce high, bounce for her too,
> Till she cry "Lover, gold-hatted,
> High-bouncing lover, I must have you!"

1927

The first Hardy Boys mystery, *The Tower Treasure,* is published

Frank and Joe Hardy clutched the grips of their motorcycles and stared in horror at the oncoming car..."He'll hit us! We'd better climb this hillside— and fast!"

So begins the first Hardy Boys book. Soon, more books were published until the series grew to include scores of titles. Each story is packed with mystery and adventure—the perfect formula for generations of boys.

Something you might remember... Series characters include the boys' parents, Fenton and Laura Hardy; Frank's girlfriend, Callie Shaw; and friends Chet Morton, Tony Prito, and Philip Cohen.

Something new to remember... The series used the pseudonym Franklin W. Dixon as the author. Various ghostwriters have written the books, all credited as Dixon.

1928

Mickey Mouse debuts in *Steamboat Willie*

I only hope that we never lose sight of one thing—
that it was all started by a mouse.
—Walt Disney, at the opening of Disneyland

Something you might remember...*Steamboat Willie* was one of the first cartoons to use sound, and it was a huge hit. Walt Disney made great use of the new sound technology. For instance, when Minnie accidentally drops her sheet music for "Turkey in the Straw," a goat eats the paper. Mickey and Minnie simply adapt, cranking the animal's tail so that the goat plays the tune. *Variety* magazine (November 21, 1928) reported that at the premiere, "Giggles came so fast...they were stumbling over each other."

Something new to remember...Mickey was originally designed by illustrator Ub Iwerks using circles in order to simplify animation. This is most noticeable in Mickey's head and ears, which in early animation always appear circular, no matter which way Mickey faces. The 🐭 has become a symbol for Mickey. Some claim that Disney often secretly places the symbol in Disney movies and around its theme parks. However, the company has never officially admitted to the existence of the "Hidden Mickeys."

1930

The first Nancy Drew mystery, *The Secret of the Old Clock,* is published

Nancy Drew, the world famous teenage sleuth, was created by Edward Stratemeyer (also the creator of the Hardy Boys series). He reportedly worried that his new heroine was "much too flip." But the feisty, confident, independent, bold, and strong Nancy Drew quickly became so popular that her books became a best-selling series for girls. Like the Hardy Boys books, the Nancy Drew books are written by various ghostwriters. Carolyn Keene is a pseudonym.

Something you might remember... Key characters include Nancy's best friends Bess Marvin and George Fayne; Nancy's father, Carson Drew; housekeeper Hannah Gruen; and Aunt Eloise. And, of course, who can forget the famous image of Nancy peering through her quizzing glass?

Something new to remember...A number of successful women have cited Nancy Drew as inspiration for their trailblazing success, including Barbara Bush, Hillary Clinton and Supreme Court Justices Sandra Day O'Connor and Sonia Sotomayor.

1931

Louis Armstrong releases "Stardust"

"Pops" or "Satchmo" remains a bigger-than-life legend in entertainment. Not only could he play the trumpet in ways that others could only try to imitate (some splitting their lips in the attempt), he was also famous for his gravelly voice and for singing scat. Pops wasn't the first to sing the scat style, but he made it popular. He was a movie star, civil rights proponent, and weaver of tall tales (especially when it came to his own life).

Something you might remember...Some of Armstrong's best-known recordings include "La Via En Rose," "What a Wonderful World," and "A Kiss to Build a Dream On."

Something new to remember...When Armstrong was a child, his father was mostly absent, creating hardship for his family. Armstrong was hired by a Jewish family, the Karnofskys, who saw his desperate needs and often treated him like one of their own, including inviting him into their home for meals. They also encouraged him to sing. As an adult, Pops wore a Star of David pendant in honor of this family.

1933

Fred Astaire and Ginger Rogers dance together in their first movie

Even though Fred Astaire and Ginger Rogers have only supporting roles in *Flying Down to Rio*, when they smoke up the screen
in a dance number called "The Carioca," it becomes their film.
This was the first of ten films the duo made together. Each film
is a delightful mixture of screwball comedy, charming romance,
and legendary dancing.

Something you might remember... Other Fred Astaire dance
partners included Rita Hayworth, Eleanor Powell, and Gracie Allen.

Something new to remember... Astaire enjoyed dancing with
Rogers, but wanted to be a solo dancer. After making *Rio*, Astaire
sent a note to his agent: "I don't mind making another picture with
her, but as for this team idea, it's out...I don't want to be bothered
with any more [partnerships]." But once the critics began to lavish
praise on the partners' dancing in *Rio*, Astaire changed his mind.

1934

First sales of Monopoly

Rainy vacation days and holidays are perfect for Monopoly. Short, long, or *very* long games have the same objective: accumulate land, buildings, and wealth while driving everyone else bankrupt. Remember the thrill of a competitor landing on Boardwalk? Or the desperate feeling of selling off property in a last-ditch attempt to avoid bankruptcy?

Something you might remember...Game tokens have included the horse and rider, thimble, wheelbarrow, Scottie dog, iron, and top hat. Board locations include Chance, No Parking, Park Place, the railroads, and the Utilities.

Something new to remember...During World War II, the Allies created a special edition of the game for POWs held by the Nazis. Hidden in the games were maps, compasses, real money, and other objects useful for escaping. Fake charity groups distributed them to the POWs. Reportedly, these escape tools were sometimes helpful. However, it's not known how effective the "Get Out of Jail Free" cards were.

1935

Count Basie begins leading his own orchestra

William "Count" Basie led his orchestra for almost fifty years, producing hits like "Jumping at the Woodside," "Cherokee," and "One O'Clock Jump." As with other royal nicknames of the day (such as Duke Ellington), Basie's moniker, "Count," quickly took hold.

Something you might remember...In 1970, the Basie orchestra and Frank Sinatra performed together in London. Sinatra later said, "I have a funny feeling that those two nights could have been my finest hour, really. It went so well; it was so thrilling and exciting."

Something new to remember..."One O'Clock Jump" was made up on the spot, during a late-night radio broadcast. With ten minutes left in the program, the group was short on material. The announcer asked Basie what the next selection would be. Basie looked at the clock and noticed it was almost 1:00 a.m. Thinking quickly, he said, "Call it 'One O'Clock Jump.'" It became one of his greatest hits.

1936

Dale Carnegie's *How to Win Friends and Influence People* is published

Over fifty million copies of Carnegie's self-help book have been sold worldwide, helping millions become more confident and successful in business and in their personal lives. For about eighty years, the book has continued to be popular. Even Soviet Union leaders were known to have bought and translated Carnegie's work.

Something you might remember...A sample taste of Carnegie's advice:

I am very fond of strawberries and cream, but I have found that for some strange reason, fish prefer worms. So when I went fishing, I didn't think about what I wanted. I thought about what they wanted. I didn't bait the hook with strawberries and cream. Rather, I dangled a worm or grasshopper in front of the fish.

Something new to remember...In a shrewd marketing move, Carnegie changed his last name from Carnagey to Carnegie, the same spelling as well-known steel magnate Andrew Carnegie.

1937

Snow White and the Seven Dwarfs premieres

When Hollywood heard that Walt Disney was creating a full-length animated film, many were convinced it would fail, labeling it "Disney's folly." But at the film's premiere in Los Angeles on December 21, 1937, it received a standing ovation from the audience, which included many Hollywood celebrities. Within a week, Disney and his dwarfs were on the cover of *Time* magazine.

Something you might remember... At the eleventh Academy Awards, Walt Disney received an honorary Oscar for the film: a full-size Oscar and seven miniatures, presented by child actress Shirley Temple.

Something new to remember...*Snow White* is based on the Grimm Brothers' fairy tale. Because it was an ancient story (and none of the dwarfs originally had names), some animators argued against the modern name Dopey. Walt Disney argued—convincingly—that because Shakespeare had used the word, Dopey was an appropriate name. There was just one problem: Shakespeare never used the word!

1937

First radio broadcast of *The Shadow*

"Who knows what evil lurks in the hearts of men?
The Shadow knows!"

nitially, the Shadow narrated the radio program *Detective Story Hour*. The character became so popular that *The Shadow: A Detective Magazine* was launched in 1931. *The Shadow* radio show premiered in 1937 with the episode, "The Death House Rescue," featuring Orson Welles (pictured) as the Shadow. The show continued on the radio until December 27, 1954.

Something you might remember...Orson Welles is the most famous voice of the Shadow, portraying him for the first year.

Something new to remember...Only on the radio does the Shadow have the ability to cloud men's minds so they cannot see him. This saved time, so that writers didn't have to explain how the Shadow was able to hide.

1938

"The War of the Worlds" radio episode airs

Presented by *Mercury Theatre on the Air,* this Halloween radio episode was broadcast on the Columbia Broadcasting System on October 30, 1938. Directed by and featuring Orson Welles (pictured), the program used fictional news bulletins, purportedly interrupting a music program, to report an alien invasion from Mars.

Something you might remember... Despite repeated notices that the broadcast was fiction, many people took it seriously. In the days that followed, angry listeners claimed the news bulletin format was especially misleading. There was an outcry of indignation directed against the program's creators and actors. Twenty-three-year-old Orson Welles couldn't have asked for better publicity.

Something new to remember... When Adolph Hitler heard about the hullabaloo, he reportedly said that the panic caused by the program was "evidence of the decadence and corrupt condition of democracy." It was these decaying democracies, however, that took down the Third Reich.

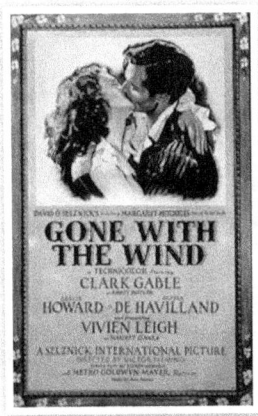

1939

Gone with the Wind premieres

Gone with the Wind is based on Margaret Mitchell's 1936 Pulitzer-winning novel portraying the American Civil War and Reconstruction from the perspective of white Southerners. The film's stars include Clark Gable, Vivien Leigh, Leslie Howard, Olivia de Havilland, and Hattie McDaniel.

Something you might remember... This was the longest and most expensive American film up to that time. It cost over $3.9 million to produce and ran for a total of three hours and forty minutes. But the film's length didn't discourage audiences. Adjusted for inflation, it is the highest earning film ever.

Something new to remember... No fine was assessed for using the word "damn" in Rhett Butler's exit line. The Motion Picture Association passed an amendment to the Production Code on November 1, 1939, just before the release of the film, making its use possible.

1939

The Wizard of Oz premieres

Flying monkeys! The Wicked Witch of the West. Glenda, the beautiful Witch of the North. A wacky wizard. A yellow brick road. An emerald city. Ruby slippers. Munchkins. Farmhands turned scarecrow, tin man, and lion. Judy Garland singing "Somewhere Over the Rainbow." All of these great memories are in the most-watched movie in history.

Something you might remember... Famous movie quotes that became a part of our culture such as: "There's no place like home."..."Toto, I've got a feeling we're not in Kansas anymore."... "I'll get you, my pretty and your little dog, too!"..."Lions and tigers and bears, oh my!"..."I'm melting! Melting!"..."Pay no attention to that man behind the curtain!"

Something new to remember... Buddy Ebsen (Jed Clampett in *The Beverly Hillbillies*) was the original Tin Man but had to give up the part because he was hospitalized in serious condition when the aluminum powder used in his makeup made him ill.

1940

First radio broadcast of Edward R. Murrow's *London After Dark*

The horrific Nazi bombing of London began on September 7, 1940, with seventy-six consecutive nights of devastation. The Germans continued to pound London on and off until May 21, 1941. Murrow's reporting from London brought Americans the news of the devastation as well as the heroics of the British people. He began each broadcast with *"This...is London,"* and ended with "Good night and good luck."

Something you might remember... Murrow's sign-off was a tribute to Londoners who, not at all certain they would see each other again, said good-bye with, "So long and good luck." In fact, a teenage future Queen Elizabeth II used a similar sign-off when she addressed British children during an October 13, 1940, radio broadcast.

Something new to remember... Murrow's former speech professor, Ida Lou Anderson, suggested the famous opening, including the emphasis on the first word.

1941

Citizen Kane premieres

Often considered to be the greatest film ever, *Citizen Kane* was as controversial when it was released as its director/cowriter/star, Orson Welles (pictured). Newspaper magnate William Randolph Hearst was convinced that the movie was about him. He was furious and prohibited any of his newspapers from mentioning the film. Welles, however, coyly claimed that Charles Foster Kane was simply a combination of personalities.

Something you might remember... Many of the main actors in the film had also worked on the *War of the Worlds*. When Kane (Welles) says, "Don't believe everything you hear on the radio," it may have been a sly reminder of that radio broadcast.

Something new to remember...*Peanuts* creator Charles M. Schulz loved this movie. His strips sometimes referred to the film. In a 1974 strip, Linus is watching TV and Lucy asks him what he is watching. Linus replies, "Citizen Kane," and Lucy says, "Rosebud was his sled."

1941

The Andrews Sisters release "Boogie Woogie Bugle Boy"

When the Andrews Sisters sang, it wasn't the big band accompanying them that drew attention. It was those three voices that sounded like trumpets, ringing out in perfect harmony. Some big band leaders resented the idea of the girls upstaging the band, but the trio was instantly popular with teens and young adults. Eventually, LaVerne, Maxene, and Patty sold over 75 million records, acted in movies, and were among the busiest artists who entertained troops during World War II.

Something you might remember...The sisters recorded forty-seven songs with Bing Crosby, including million-sellers, "Get Your Kicks on Route 66," "Pistol Packin' Mama," "Don't Fence Me In," and "South America, Take It Away."

Something new to remember...Legend has it the Andrews Sisters were so popular in Germany that during World War II their records were sometimes smuggled in, labeled as "Hitler's Marching Songs."

1942

Casablanca premieres

It seemed unlikely that *Casablanca* would become a classic. This was Humphrey Bogart's first romantic lead and he had never worked with Ingrid Bergman. Screenwriters were coming and going, and the writing was just staying ahead of the film's production. But the powerful chemistry between Bogart and Bergman (both pictured), along with the acting of Claude Rains, Peter Lorre, and Dooley Wilson created a classic.

Something you might remember... Rick doesn't ever actually say, "Play it again, Sam." He really says, "You played it for her, you can play it for me...If she can stand it, I can. Play it!"

Something new to remember... In the 1980s, the film's script was sent to various studios with its original title, *Everybody Comes to Rick's.* Some script readers recognized it but many did not—and panned it as "not good enough." Others claimed it was "too dated," with "too much dialogue" and "not enough sex."

1942

Bing Crosby releases "White Christmas"

I'm dreaming of a white Christmas,
Just like the ones I used to know.
Where the treetops glisten,
And children listen
To hear sleigh bells in the snow.

Written by Irving Berlin and released during wartime, Bing Crosby's recording became the best-selling single ever. In fact, the song had to be re-recorded just a few years later because the master recording was worn out. Even Crosby (pictured) didn't recognize the song's potential. As recording wrapped up, he is reported to have simply said, "I don't think we have any problems with that one."

Something you might remember... The 1954 movie, *White Christmas*, stars Bing Crosby, Danny Kaye, and Rosemary Clooney.

Something new to remember... The song is a Filipino favorite and can be heard everywhere on the islands when Christmas celebrations begin—in September!

1942

Yankee Doodle Dandy premieres

James Cagney (pictured) played some of Hollywood's toughest guys, including Tom Powers in *The Public Enemy* and Rocky Sullivan in *Angels with Dirty Faces.* But he was also a great dancer. *Yankee Doodle Dandy,* the biographical musical of George M. Cohan, gave Cagney the opportunity to highlight his dancing and singing. Today, the film is regarded as one of the greats and of all of Cagney's films, it was his personal favorite.

Something you might remember... When director Michael Curtiz shot the death scene of Cohan's father, it wasn't just the actors who were crying. Reportedly, Curtiz cried too.

Something new to remember... The film was a family affair of sorts. Actress Jeanne Cagney, who played Cohan's sister in the film, was Cagney's real life sister. Associate producer William Cagney was Cagney's brother.

1946

It's a Wonderful Life premieres

Produced and directed by Frank Capra, the film stars Jimmy Stewart, Donna Reed (both pictured), and Lionel Barrymore (Potter). It's the ultimate feel-good movie and was Stewart's favorite. Yet, it also explores the dark side of the human experience: crushed dreams, a father worked to death, and standing still while others forge ahead.

Something you might remember... When George prays in Martini's bar, Stewart said that he was so emotional, his sobs were real.

Something new to remember... Seneca Falls, New York, claims to be the inspiration for Bedford Falls. Annually, the town holds an It's a Wonderful Life festival. In fact, both Stewart and Reed came from small towns (Stewart from Indiana, Pennsylvania, and Reed from Denison, Iowa). During filming, Barrymore challenged Reed's small-town credentials, betting she couldn't milk a cow. A cow was brought on set, which Reed easily milked.

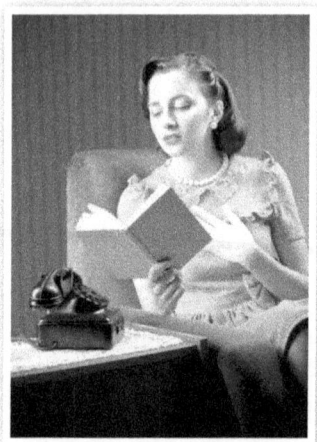

1946

Dr. Spock's *The Common Sense Book of Baby and Child Care* is published

"Trust yourself. You know more than you think you do." Those are the first lines of a book that has sales of over 50 million copies. After World War II, millions of couples became parents for the first time—the baby boom. These new parents were searching for updated advice on raising children. Spock's book spoke to them in a friendly manner, encouraging parents to believe in themselves and trust their instincts.

Something you might remember...Spock has been accused of advocating permissiveness—which he strongly denied, saying, "I've always advised parents to give their children firm, clear leadership and to ask for cooperation and politeness in return."

Something new to remember...Spock was a member of the 1924 Yale Eight gold medal US Olympic rowing team. He continued to be an avid rower throughout his life.

1949

Billy Graham's Los Angeles Crusade

Graham preached for over sixty years and witnessed to presidents, gangsters, and celebrities. It was this 1949 crusade that made Graham a national figure. Newspaper tycoon William Randolph Hearst heard about Graham and ordered his editors to "puff [promote] Graham." Because of the publicity, 350,000 souls attended Graham's services over the next several weeks.

Something you might remember... Actress Jane Russell attended the crusade and said, "I remember wheeling a former soldier, wounded in the war, down that sawdust aisle to meet Billy and receive the Lord...I remember how happy it made me, and him."

Something new to remember... Graham indicated that he learned about the "Puff Graham" telegram from Hearst's sons, who told him that their father, along with his mistress Marion Davies, came to the revival in disguise.

1950

First *Peanuts* cartoon strip is published

Peanuts' national debut was on October 2, 1950. Over the next fifty years, it became the most popular comic strip in history. At its peak, the strip was published in seventy-five countries, with an estimated readership of 355 million. Characters include Charlie Brown, Lucy, Linus, Snoopy, Peppermint Patty, and Sally. Charles M. Schulz (pictured) continued the strip until his health made it impossible. He died February 12, 2000, just one day before the last original *Peanuts* strip ran in papers.

Something you might remember... It's ironic that the world's most successful comic strip features such an unsuccessful character. Good Ol' Charlie Brown tries so hard but can never fly a kite, win a baseball game, or kick a football. And Lucy is his psychiatrist.

Something new to remember... Early on, United Features changed the strip's name from *Li'l Folks* to *Peanuts*, after the *Howdy Doody* peanut gallery. Schulz never liked the title, believing that for all its humor, his comic strip had "dignity."

1951

First broadcast of *I Love Lucy*

I Love Lucy (originally airing from October 15, 1951, to May 6, 1957) gave millions of Americans aching belly laughs as Lucy's slapstick comedy entertained a nation just tuning into television. For four of its six seasons, it was the most popular show on TV.

Something you might remember... Lucy's pregnancy during the second season became part of the story line. On the actual day of Lucy's cesarean delivery, "Lucy Goes to the Hospital" was watched by the largest TV audience up to that time, even topping the following day's coverage of Dwight D. Eisenhower's inauguration.

Something new to remember... Since the debut of *I Love Lucy,* the show has always aired on TV somewhere. Want to know a secret? Lucy wasn't really a redhead. According to Lucy's hairdresser, Irma Kusely, the star's true hair color was golden apricot.

1951

A Streetcar Named Desire premieres

"*Stella! Hey, Stella!*"
The film is an adaptation of Tennessee Williams' stage play. Vivian Leigh plays Blanche, an aging, mentally unstable aristocrat who had to leave her home because of moral failings. She runs to her pregnant sister Stella (Kim Hunter) in New Orleans. Stella's crude husband, Stanley Kowalski (Marlon Brando), hates Blanche. Meanwhile, Blanche and Mitch (Karl Malden) begin a romance, until Stanley tells Mitch what Blanche did. Stanley finally destroys Blanche's sanity in a brutal confrontation.

Something you might remember... Blanche says, "I have always depended on the kindness of strangers."

Something new to remember... As the film progresses, the set of the Kowalski apartment actually gets smaller, heightening the sense of Blanche's claustrophobia and panic.

1952

Singin' in the Rain premieres

The film was only a modest hit when it first was released, but is now regarded as one of the best musicals ever. *Singin' in the Rain* was directed by Gene Kelly (with Stanley Donen); it stars Gene Kelly (along with Donald O'Connor and Debbie Reynolds); and it was choreographed by Gene Kelly. It is truly Gene Kelly throughout. The songs were written prior to the script, so the writers had to create a story that fit the songs. Reportedly, one of the screenwriters had bought a house in Hollywood from a former silent film star whose career ended when movies became "talkies." This became the story line.

Something you might remember... The film's songs include "Fit as a Fiddle (And Ready for Love)," "Temptation," "All I Do is Dream of You," "Make 'Em Laugh," and "Moses Supposes."

Something new to remember... Though Debbie Reynolds looks fantastic tap dancing, Gene Kelly didn't like the way it sounded and dubbed his own tapping for the soundtrack.

1952

High Noon premieres

Gary Cooper (pictured) was about thirty years older than Grace Kelly, but in *High Noon* they are husband and wife. The film purports to be in "real time," from 10:40 a.m. until 12:15 p.m., about the same length of time as the film. It is a story of standing up to evil even when others want to accommodate or surrender. Will Kane (Cooper) tries in vain to rally the townspeople to defend themselves and stand up to the threats of an outlaw, but they refuse to put themselves at risk. Eventually, he alone saves a town that doesn't deserve to be saved.

Something you might remember... No one is willing to risk themselves to stand up to the outlaw oppressor: not the deputy, the judge, the business community, nor the politician.

Something new to remember... This is reportedly one of Bill Clinton's favorite films. He is said to have watched it over fifteen times while he was president.

1953

Marilyn Monroe stars in
Gentlemen Prefer Blondes

Monroe (pictured) wasn't the first to play Lorelei, the diamond-loving showgirl. The 1925 novel by Anita Loos, *Gentlemen Prefer Blondes: The Intimate Diary of a Professional Lady,* was adapted for stage as far back as 1926, and then as a 1928 silent movie (now lost). In 1949, Carol Channing played Lorelei on Broadway. While the 1953 film featured both Jane Russell and Marilyn Monroe, it is Monroe's role—and her pink dress—that is most remembered.

Something you might remember... Loos wrote a sequel to her novel, *But Gentlemen Marry Brunettes*, which was the title of a 1955 movie, also with Jane Russell.

Something new to remember... Monroe's pink dress has been copied by Madonna, Nicole Kidman, Anna Nicole Smith, and Christina Aguilera. When told she was not the main star of the film, Marilyn Monroe was quoted as saying, "Well whatever I am, I'm still the blonde."

1954

Seven Brides for Seven Brothers premieres

Flaming red hair, tons of manliness, kidnappings, shotgun weddings, great vocals, and some really fine dancing—all set in 1850 Oregon. That is *Seven Brides for Seven Brothers*. Depending on your perspective, the film either celebrates masculinity or is a commentary on the oppression of women. Or maybe, it's just fun. The film stars Jane Powell and Howard Keel (who later played Miss Ellie's second husband, Clayton Farlow, on *Dallas*).

Something you might remember... One of the brides (Dorcas) was played by Julie Newmar. Newmar, a classically trained ballerina, couldn't show off her abilities in this film because her dance partner, Jeff Richards, was a former baseball player with limited dancing skills. Newmar later played Catwoman in the TV version of *Batman*.

Something new to remember... The script is based on the short story, "The Sobbin' Women," which itself is based on Plutarch's *Life of Romulus*.

1954

First broadcast of *Lassie*

The character Lassie was introduced in a December 17, 1938, *Saturday Evening Post* story by Eric Knight. It's possible, however, that the idea of Lassie can be traced to an 1859 story, "The Half-brothers," which featured a collie rescuing a freezing boy. In 1940, Knight published a novel based on his earlier magazine article. Knight's book was adapted in 1943 for the film *Lassie Come Home*. The TV series ran from September 12, 1954, to March 24, 1973, always on Sunday evenings.

Something you might remember... While Lassie is a female, all of the collies playing her on TV were male, because female dogs frequently shed and the larger male dogs were thought to be more telegenic.

Something new to remember... Ruth Martin (Timmy's mother from 1958–1964) was famously played by June Lockhart (pictured). But before Lockhart, Cloris Leachman played Mrs. Martin.

1954

First broadcast of the *Tonight* show

In 1953, Steve Allen (pictured) pioneered a late-night TV program on New York's WNBC. The show then went national as *Tonight*.

Something you might remember... On February 11, 1960, host Jack Paar walked off the show because censors deleted a joke. Announcer Hugh Downs had to finish the broadcast. When Paar returned on March 7, he came out, turned to the camera and said, "As I was saying before I was interrupted."

Something new to remember... The censored joke? A polite English lady visits Switzerland. She inquires about the location of the "WC" (the water closet). The Swiss think she means the "Wayside Chapel." They leave her a note: "The WC is nine miles from your room and can hold 229 people. It is only open on Sunday and Thursday. It may interest you to know that my daughter met her future husband at the WC and was married there. I shall happily reserve the best seat for you, so you will be seen by everyone."

1955

James Dean dies in a high-speed automobile accident

His movie roles were that of the ultimate bad boy—and his early death froze this image in time. James Byron Dean's entire movie career consisted of just three films: *East of Eden, Rebel without a Cause,* and *Giant.* Only *Rebel* was released prior to Dean's death. *East of Eden* was released within a month of his death. *Giant* was released the next year.

Something you might remember...Dean's first acting job was in a 1950 Pepsi-Cola TV commercial. The next year, he debuted on TV as the apostle John in *Hill Number One.*

Something new to remember...Ironically, just before his death, Dean filmed a National Safety Council safe-driving public service announcement. Dean warns about the dangers of driving fast on a highway. Instead of ending with the standard phrase, "The life you save may be your own," Dean quips, "The life you might save might be mine." The PSA was released after Dean's death.

1955

McDonald's Corporation founded

Brothers Richard and Maurice McDonald opened their first restaurant in 1940. In 1948, they began selling hamburgers, using the Speedee Service System (developed by White Castle). Over the next few years, they franchised a couple of restaurants and were comfortable. Everything changed, however, when Ray Kroc got involved and eventually purchased the chain from the McDonald's brothers. Kroc, a true innovator, began franchising in earnest and growth exploded.

Something you might remember... According to one survey, 96 percent of all school-age children in the United States recognize Ronald McDonald, second only to Santa Claus. Who played the first representation of Ronald McDonald in 1963 TV ads? Willard Scott, the future NBC *Today* show weatherman!

Something new to remember... There are over 34,000 McDonald's restaurants in over 115 countries. McDonald's serves over 60 million customers daily.

1955

First broadcast of *The Honeymooners*

Only thirty-nine episodes of this show were ever produced. Yet, it is one of the great early TV classics. The show features Ralph Kramden (Jackie Gleason), a New York bus driver and his best friend, Edward "Ed" Norton (Art Carney), who works in the sewers. Kramden's exasperated wife, Alice (Audrey Meadows), is always there to pick him up when he falls. And Norton's wife, Trixie (Joyce Randolph), keeps Norton in line.

Something you might remember... The window in the Kramdens' apartment has a choice view of fire escapes and other windows. Except when the fire escapes mistakenly aren't there— sometimes alternating within the same episode.

Something new to remember... The show was shot "as live" (filmed before an audience, edited and broadcast later). If you ever notice Jackie Gleason patting his stomach, it was a sign that he had forgotten his line.

1955

First TV broadcast of *Gunsmoke*

Gunsmoke began as a radio program in 1952. Set in Dodge City, it was an adult western, with some of the most explicit content of its time, including violent crimes and opium addicts. The "realism" continued during its twenty seasons and 635 episodes on TV. The *Los Angeles Times* called the show the American *Iliad* and *Odyssey*.

Something you might remember... Cast members and the show's scores of guests included James Arness (US Marshal Matt Dillon), Milburn Stone (Doc Adams), Amanda Blake (Kitty Russell), Dennis Weaver (Chester B. Goode), Ken Curtis (Festus Haggen), Burt Reynolds, Bette Davis, James Brown, Barbara Eden, and Ron Howard.

Something new to remember... During a ratings slump in 1967, the program was moved to Monday evenings, replacing *Gilligan's Island*, which was cancelled. It worked; ratings quickly rebounded.

1955

Oklahoma! premieres

The original Broadway production (which opened March 31, 1943, and ran for an unprecedented 2,212 performances) was the first musical from the team of Richard Rodgers and Oscar Hammerstein. The setting is the Oklahoma Territory, just before 1907 when Oklahoma became a state. The film stars Gordon MacRae (Curly), Shirley Jones (pictured, Laurey), and Rod Steiger (Jud Fry). It was Shirley Jones' film debut.

Something you might remember... From start to finish, the film is full of fun lyrics, lofty music and wide open vocals such as the title song, "Oklahoma" and "Oh What a Beautiful Mornin'."

Something new to remember... The burlesque performers in Laurie's dream sequence were also cast members who had other roles as respectable members of the community. Also because filmmakers could not find a professional dancer who looked like Rod Steiger, he actually did all of his own dancing. Steiger later said it was one of the most difficult challenges of his career.

1955

Blackboard Jungle premieres featuring "Rock Around the Clock"

"Rock Around the Clock" was a minor hit when it was first released in 1954 by Bill Haley and the Comets as the B-side to "Thirteen Women (and Only One Man in Town)." Peter Ford, the son of *Blackboard Jungle* star Glenn Ford, had the song in his record collection, and it was chosen for the opening credits of the movie. Once the film was released, a million copies of "Rock Around the Clock" were sold in a single month.

Something you might remember..."Rock Around the Clock" was the first rock 'n' roll song to top *Billboard's* pop charts. The Comets appeared on the Ed Sullivan show in August 1955, becoming the first act to perform a rock 'n' roll song on a national TV program.

Something new to remember... The song has been covered by many, including Pat Boone, Chubby Checker, Tiny Tim, the Isley Brothers, the Platters, and Mae West.

1955

First broadcast of *Captain Kangaroo*

B ob Keeshan (pictured, left) based his show on "the warm relationship between grandparents and children." Captain Kangaroo's name came from his large pockets on his jacket. The original dark jacket became a red jacket with the advent of color TV. In addition to his role as the Captain, Keeshan also played the Town Clown, a throwback to his appearances on *Howdy Doody* as Clarabell. Hugh "Lumpy" Brannum (pictured, right) played Mr. Green Jeans, among other characters.

Something you might remember...Classic memories from the show include: Mr. Moose and his shower of Ping-Pong balls, Tom Terrific, the Magic Drawing Board, and the Captain's book readings, including *Curious George, Stone Soup,* and *Mike Mulligan and His Steam Shovel.*

Something new to remember... When Bob Keeshan began the show, he wore makeup that made him look older for his grandfatherly character. The show was on the air for so many seasons that by the end of its run, he was wearing makeup, including various hairpieces, to make himself look younger.

1956

The Ten Commandments premieres

Director Cecil B. DeMille's epic biblical story of the Exodus stars Charlton Heston as Moses (pictured), Yul Brynner as Pharaoh, Anne Baxter as Nefretiri, and Edward G. Robinson as Dathan. This was DeMille's last film and is narrated by DeMille himself. But who is the voice of God at the burning bush? DeMille? Heston? Someone else? The voice is too heavily modified to identify. Only DeMille and his sound editor knew for sure, but they are both deceased. Of course God knows, but so far He isn't saying.

Something you might remember...DeMille had a heart attack during filming when he climbed 130 feet to check on a faulty camera perched atop a giant gate. Reportedly, just two days later, he returned to directing.

Something new to remember...The last line of the film, "Proclaim liberty throughout all the land, unto all the inhabitants thereof," is from the Bible's book of Leviticus. The same verse is engraved on the Liberty Bell.

1956

Elvis gyrates on *The Ed Sullivan Show*

Initially, Sullivan didn't want the controversial Elvis on his show. But locked in an intense ratings battle with Steve Allen, Sullivan relented. Explaining his change of heart, Sullivan said, "What I said then was off the reports I'd heard. I hadn't even seen the guy. Seeing the kinescopes, I don't know what the fuss was all about." Elvis had previously appeared on *The Milton Berle Show.* Sullivan's reaction to that performance was, "I don't know why everybody picked on Presley. The whole show was dirty and vulgar."

Something you might remember...On Sullivan's show, Elvis performed "Don't Be Cruel," "Love Me Tender," "Ready Teddy," and "You Ain't Nothin' But a Hound Dog."

Something new to remember...Since Sullivan was recovering from a near fatal automobile accident, Charles Laughton guest-hosted this particular show. He mistakenly introduced Presley as "Elvin Presley."

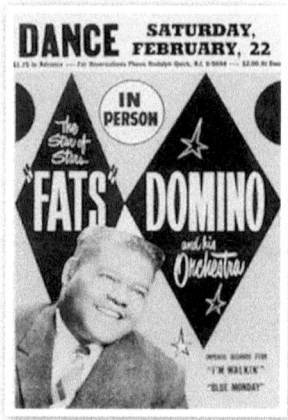

1956

Fats Domino releases "Blueberry Hill"

"Blueberry Hill" has been covered by many artists, including Louis Armstrong, Elvis, Little Richard, Gene Autry, Andy Williams, the Glenn Miller Orchestra, Conway Twitty, The Everly Brothers, Led Zepplin, Loretta Lynn, Jerry Lee Lewis, the Beach Boys, and Elton John. But it was Fats Domino (pictured) who made the song an international hit and a rock 'n' roll anthem. "The Fat Man" took the song to number two on the *Billboard* Top 40, making it the biggest hit of his career.

Something you might remember... Fats sold over 65 million records, with other hits like "Ain't That a Shame" and "Blue Monday." He sold more records than any fifties rocker except Elvis.

Something new to remember... Russian tough guy and Prime Minister Vladimir Putin performed the song on December 10, 2010, before a star-studded audience at a children's charity dinner in St. Petersburg. The video went viral.

1957

American Bandstand, hosted by Dick Clark, goes national

For thirty years, Dick Clark (pictured) hosted *American Bandstand,* giving rock 'n' roll a clean-cut image that helped mainstream America welcome the new music into its homes. Each show featured dancing teenagers and an appearance by a popular artist or group. Over the years, hundreds of acts appeared on the show, including Bill Haley and His Comets, Fats Domino, ABBA, the Supremes, the Doors, Marvin Gaye, and Chuck Berry.

Something you might remember... During the "Rate-a-Record" segment of the show, Clark would ask audience members to rate records and give their opinion of the song. In a surprise move, comedians Cheech and Chong once appeared as record-raters.

Something new to remember... In all of the years he hosted the show, there was only one performer who ever cohosted with Clark—Donna Summer.

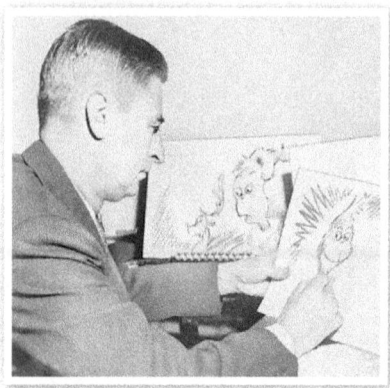

1957

Dr. Seuss publishes *The Cat in the Hat*

Theodore Geisel (pictured) wrote *The Cat in the Hat* in response to a 1954 *Life* magazine article criticizing the "pallid readers" used in the nation's schools. Geisel was asked by the director of Houghton Mifflin's education division to write and illustrate a story that "first-graders can't put down." He told Geisel to limit the book's vocabulary to 225 words that every first-grader should know.

Something you might remember... The book uses only 236 different words. Dr. Seuss thought writing such a book would be relatively easy, but it took him a year and a half. He was used to making up and experimenting with words, so limiting himself to a list of words was challenging.

Something new to remember... The first edition of the book cost about $2. According to the *Children's Picturebook Price Guide, 2006-2007*, a first edition copy of the *Cat in the Hat* could now fetch $4,000.

1957

First broadcast of *Leave It to Beaver*

Sponsors didn't like the original show title, *Wally and the Beaver*, worried that viewers would mistake the show for a nature program. But great performances from Hugh Beaumont as Ward Cleaver, Barbara Billingsley as June Cleaver, Tony Dow as Wally, and Jerry Mathers as the Beaver, meant that no one would ever make that mistake.

Something you might remember... In the very first episode, Wally and Beaver try to hide a baby alligator in their toilet tank. Network censors didn't approve the episode in time for the program's debut, so it aired later. Leave It to Beaver became the first American TV program to show a toilet tank.

Something new to remember...A fidgety Jerry Mathers wore his Cub Scout uniform to his audition, telling casting personnel he was eager to leave for his den meeting. The cuteness factor was too much. He got the part.

1958

Chuck Berry releases "Johnny B. Goode"

Few musicians have influenced rock 'n' roll like Chuck Berry. His furious guitar work and on-stage persona shaped both the music and the style of the new genre. Eric Clapton has said, "'If you wanted to play rock and roll...you would end up playing like Chuck...There's not a lot of other ways to play rock and roll other than the way Chuck plays it."

Something you might remember... The character Johnny B. Goode appears in other songs by Berry, including "Bye Bye Johnny" and "Johnny B. Blues." He even released an album, *Concerto in B. Goode.*

Something new to remember..."Johnny B. Goode" is on the golden records placed on the *Voyager 1* and *2* spacecraft, which have now traveled to the edge of our solar system. These records contain some of humanity's greatest music. Can you imagine the reaction when some far-flung civilization hears Chuck Berry for the first time?

1958

The Hula-Hoop fad

The Wham-O Mfg. Co. was started in 1948 by college graduates Arthur "Spud" Melin and Richard Knerr. The duo initially worked out of a garage in South Pasadena, California. In 1957, Wham-O began manufacturing their "Hula-Hoops" with Marlex, a new plastic. After an intense local marketing campaign, including giveaways, the Hula-Hoop fad took off. Twenty-five million Hula-Hoops were sold in less than four months. By the end of 1959, over one hundred million hoops had been sold.

Something you might remember... Wham-O also markets the Frisbee, the Slip 'N Slide, the Super Ball, and Silly String.

Something new to remember... The name Wham-O is based on the comic book sound of a target being hit. When the missiles shooting from the company's first product, an ash wood slingshot, hit their target, it reminded the founders of the sound.

1959

Buddy Holly is killed in a plane crash

His music exploded on the pop scene and transformed rock 'n' roll. But at only twenty-two years of age, Buddy Holly was killed in a plane crash. Holly's new wife was pregnant and his manager was mishandling royalties. Holly needed some quick money and agreed to play the Winter Dance Party tour of the Midwest. It was during a snowstorm that Holly, Ritchie Valens, and "Big Bopper" Richardson were killed. Teens around the country were shaken. As Don McLean later sang, it really was the day the music died.

Something you might remember... Inspired by the group the Spiders, Holly's band wanted an insect name. They settled on the Crickets because, according to bassist Joe Mauldin, crickets "chirp and all that stuff."

Something new to remember... John Lennon once said that Holly's influence on the Beatles was so significant that they chose their name partly in homage to the Crickets.

1959

Barbie is introduced to America

Barbara, the daughter of Mattel cofounders Elliot and Ruth Handler, enjoyed playing with paper dolls that she pretended were college students, cheerleaders, and adults. At the time, most dolls were infants or toddlers. Ruth saw the need for a teenage doll, so that young girls could "experiment with the future." Barbie, the Teen-Age Fashion Model, was introduced at the American International Toy Fair on March 9, 1959, Barbie's official birthday. Why "Barbie"? Naturally, Ruth named the doll for her daughter Barbara.

Something you might remember...The company's name, Mattel, is a combination of the first names of the male co-founders, Matt Matson and Elliot Handler. Like so many other successful businesses, Mattel also began in a garage workshop.

Something new to remember...In 2012, Mattel announced that Barbie was running for president. Her 2012 pink campaign skirt suit was designed by award-winning fashion designer Chris Benz.

1959

First Broadcast of *The Twilight Zone*

Series creator Rod Serling was already a popular TV writer known for controversial material such as *Noon on Doomsday* (about the murder of Emmett Till). Frustrated by network censorship, Serling used the aliens and supernatural occurrences of *The Twilight Zone* as cover for his ideas.

Something you might remember... The series featured well-known stars at the time (such as Joan Blondell, Ann Blyth, Buster Keaton, and Burgess Meredith) as well as young actors (including William Shatner, Leonard Nimoy, Elizabeth Montgomery, and Robert Redford).

Something new to remember...A real-life *Twilight Zone* moment occurred in 1962 in the town of Valdese, North Carolina. A Duke Power crew reversed a forty-thousand-volt line running to manufacturing plants. Machinery began running in reverse. At a spinning mill, spindles unwound at twelve thousand rpms. At another facility a conveyor belt that delivered coal to furnaces reversed. And at a bakery, baked loaves returned to the oven. The incident was featured in a 1965 *Twilight Zone* comic book.

1960

The Magnificent Seven premieres

The film is based on the 1954 Japanese film, *Seven Samurai,* and features an incredible cast of male actors. A movie with so much testosterone, a compelling story line, and a soaring musical score just had to be one of the great Hollywood westerns. Its theme song was even made into a marching band arrangement and was frequently played at Friday night football games.

Something you might remember... The gunfighters who become heroes are played by Yul Brynner, Steve McQueen, Charles Bronson, James Coburn, Robert Vaughn, Brad Dexter, and Horst Buchholz. Eli Wallach plays the bandit leader.

Something new to remember... Brynner recommended McQueen for the film but later regretted this. He realized that McQueen was drawing attention to himself in many scenes, through small actions like shaking shotgun shells or taking off his hat to check the sun. Reportedly, Brynner (five feet ten inches) insisted he always appear taller than McQueen (five feet nine and a half inches), so at one point he made a mound of dirt and stood on it for their shot together. McQueen is said to have kicked at the mound every time he passed by.

1960

First broadcast of *The Andy Griffith Show*

The show initially aired from October 3, 1960, to April 1, 1968. Griffith plays the sheriff of Mayberry who lives with his son, Opie (later *Happy Days* star Ron Howard) and his Aunt Bee (Frances Bavier). He is assisted by his hilariously inept deputy, Barney Fife (Don Knotts). Originally, Griffith played the sheriff like a character he had developed for his successful stand-up comedy routine. However, after working with Knotts for just a short time, Griffith realized it would be better TV for the sheriff to be the straight man.

Something you might remember…Even when the show first aired it was meant to be nostalgic, with the feel of rural life in the 1930s.

Something new to remember…The show often used some of the Atlanta set from *Gone with the Wind*. In several episodes, the old Atlanta train station can be seen at the end of the street.

1960

First broadcast of *The Flintstones*

D o the main characters in *The Flintstones* remind you of characters from another famous TV show? Maybe...*The Honeymooners?* Fred and Wilma Flintstone were inspired by Ralph and Alice Kramden, while Barney and Betty Rubble were inspired by Ed and Trixie Norton. Jackie Gleason certainly saw the resemblance. Gleason wanted to sue Hanna-Barbera because of the resemblance, but then though better of it—not wishing to be known as the guy who knocked Fred Flintstone off the air. (By the way, check out the similarities between Yogi Bear and Ed Norton!)

Something you might remember... The cute factor was provided by Pebbles, Bamm-Bamm, and Dino. Well-known guests with Stone-Age names included Cary Granite, Dinah Saur, Ann Margrock, Stony Curtis, and Perry Masonry.

Something new to remember... Barney was voiced by Mel Blanc. For an entire season (1961–1962) the show was taped in Mel Blanc's bedroom because Blanc was in a full body cast recovering from a car crash.

1960

First broadcast of *The Dick Van Dyke Show*

Starring Dick Van Dyke and Mary Tyler Moore as Rob and Laura Petrie, the show portrays the working life of TV comedy writers. As Moore grew in her role—and became more popular—story lines increasingly featured the Petrie family.

Something you might remember... Mary Tyler Moore created a fashion craze by wearing capri pants on the show. At first, the network insisted she wear dresses. But Moore argued that most of the housewives she knew wore pants. The network gave in a little, but still insisted on a certain number of skirt scenes in each episode. They relented, however, when an episode showed Laura walking into the kitchen wearing capris and, due to editing and multiple takes, immediately returning wearing a skirt.

Something new to remember... Johnny Carson was a runner-up to play Rob Petrie. What if...?

1961

West Side Story premieres

West Side Story is an adaptation of the 1957 Broadway musical by the same name, itself an adaptation of William Shakespeare's *Romeo and Juliet.* The film's musical score is magical, its plot intense, and the dancing spectacular. It stars Natalie Wood (pictured), Richard Beymer, Russ Tamblyn, Rita Moreno, and George Chakiris. Both Wood and Beymer attempted to do their own singing, but they ended up having to be dubbed (not an unusual arrangement in Hollywood). Marni Nixon dubbed for Wood. She also dubbed some of the vocals for Marilyn Monroe in *Gentlemen Prefer Blondes.*

Something you might remember... The Jets and Sharks were lovable, yet violent. The film won ten Academy Awards, including Best Picture, Best Director, and Best Original Score.

Something new to remember... During production, dancers reportedly wore out two hundred pairs of shoes and split twenty-seven pairs of pants.

1962

To Kill a Mockingbird premieres

Someone once said, "When I finished watching this movie, I felt like I was a better person." It stars Mary Badham (Scout), Gregory Peck (pictured, Atticus Finch), Brock Peters (pictured, Tom Robinson), and Robert Duvall (Boo Radley). For the rest of his life, Peck heard from people touched by the film. In 1997 he said, "I recently sat at a dinner next to a woman who saw it when she was fourteen years old, and she said it changed her life. I hear things like that all the time."

Something you might remember... The American Film Institute named Atticus Finch the greatest movie hero of the twentieth century.

Something new to remember... Those who really knew Peck felt that playing Atticus Finch gave Peck the opportunity to "play himself." In fact, at Peck's funeral, Brock Peters said, "To my friend Gregory Peck; to my friend Atticus Finch: *Vaya con Dios.*"

1962

Dr. No premieres

His name? "Bond. James Bond." Starring Sean Connery (pictured), *Dr. No* was the first film in the Bond series. There have now been over twenty additional Bond films with a combined box office gross of over $8 billion. It's estimated that a quarter of all of the people in the world have seen at least one Bond film. The movies are based on author Ian Fleming's James Bond books. And although 007 is larger-than-life in the movies, Fleming's books portray him as a blander Bond.

Something you might remember... Just before Queen Elizabeth II entered the stadium for the 2012 London Olympics, a video was shown of the Queen and the most recent Bond (Daniel Craig) as her escort. The two were shown flying by military helicopter and—purportedly—parachuting into the stadium.

Something new to remember... Sean Connery wore a toupee in all of his James Bond movies. Connery is also terrified of spiders and needed a stuntman for the tarantula scene in *Dr. No.*

1962

Walter Cronkite becomes *CBS Evening News* anchor

Cronkite began his career as a reporter during the 1930s. In 1950, Edward R. Murrow recruited him to the CBS television news team. After distinguishing himself as a reporter, Cronkite became the *CBS Evening News* anchorman. He remained anchor for nineteen years and was often referred to as "the most trusted man in America."

Something you might remember... Cronkite's career as CBS anchor spanned major world-changing events like the Cuban missile crisis; the assassinations of John F. Kennedy, Robert F. Kennedy, and Martin Luther King Jr.; the Vietnam War; and the moon landing.

Something new to remember... During World War II, reporter Cronkite was selected to fly on B-17 Flying Fortress bombing raids over Germany. During one mission, he reportedly fired a machine gun at a German fighter.

And that's the way it is.

1962

Johnny Carson begins hosting
The Tonight Show

Johnny Carson's TV career began in 1949 on Omaha Nebraska's WOW. He hosted *The Squirrel's Nest* which, among other regular features, included Carson interviewing rooftop pigeons at the courthouse who had allegedly witnessed political corruption. In 1955, he appeared on *The Jack Benny Show*, imitating Benny's mannerisms and claiming that Benny had imitated him. When Jack Paar left the *Tonight Show* (for real), Carson (pictured, right with Groucho Marx) became host.

Something you might remember... While with *The Red Skelton Show*, Carson triumphantly filled in for the host when, just an hour before the live show aired, Skelton knocked himself out rehearsing a slapstick routine.

Something new to remember... Carson had an undefeated amateur boxing record while in the Navy during World War II. He also successfully sued a portable toilet company that wanted to use the name, "Here's Johnny Portable Toilets, Inc."

1963

Beach Boys release "Surfin' U.S.A."

It was the Beach Boys' first top ten single and the beginning of a wave of top forty hits during the 1960s, second only to the Beatles. In fact, both groups were creative competitors. According to Paul McCartney, the *Sgt. Pepper's* LP was the group's response to the Beach Boys' *Pet Sounds* project. *Pet Sounds* reportedly was Brian Wilson's response to the Fab Four's *Rubber Soul* album.

Something you might remember…In addition to the title track, the album features "Farmer's Daughter," "Shut Down," "Lonely Sea," and "Finders Keepers."

Something new to remember…The melody of "Surfin' U.S.A." was determined in court to be virtually the same as Chuck Berry's "Sweet Little Sixteen." The lyrics are also very similar to Bobby Rydell's 1959 hit, "Kissin' Time"—which also borrowed heavily from Berry's song. As a result of the court decision, Berry was given cowriting credit and royalties for "Surfin' U.S.A."

1964

"Ladies and Gentlemen, the Beatles!"

Ed Sullivan reportedly crossed paths with the Beatles in 1963 at London's Heathrow airport. He was stunned by the thousands of crazed fans there to welcome the group. Sullivan's show business instinct told him this was Elvis all over again. He struck a deal with the band that would give them maximum exposure: The Beatles would appear three consecutive Sundays, for very little money, but receive top billing. The British Invasion was under way.

Something you might remember... In 1966 and 1967, the band provided promotional clips of *Paperback Writer, Penny Lane,* and *Strawberry Fields Forever* for exclusive broadcast on Sullivan's show.

Something new to remember...A month before their *Ed Sullivan* appearance, Jack Paar broadcast a filmed performance of the Beatles on his NBC show, *The Jack Paar Program.* The film clip showed the band performing "She Loves You," accompanied by screaming teenage girls.

1964

Mary Poppins premieres

Few movie characters have made an entrance like Mary Poppins. With her open umbrella catching the east wind, she easily glides down from her cloud to the Banks' home. Julie Andrews won an Academy Award for Best Actress. Dick Van Dyke was unforgettable as Bert the chimney sweep. Walt Disney felt this was one of his best films, but it almost didn't happen. It took Disney twenty-three years to convince *Mary Poppins* author P. L. Travers to sell him the film rights. She finally relented in 1961.

Something you might remember…The film's classic songs include "A Spoonful of Sugar," "Chim Chim Cher-ee," "Let's Go Fly a Kite," and "Feed the Birds."

Something new to remember…Van Dyke also played Mr. Dawes Sr. (the decrepit bank manager who dies laughing). He really wanted the extra role, even offering to play the part for free. Disney was familiar with Van Dyke, and offered him the part of Bert without an audition. But Disney insisted he audition for the role of Mr. Dawes.

1964

My Fair Lady premieres

*M*y *Fair Lady* is based on the Broadway production by the same name. The stage version in turn is based on George Bernard Shaw's 1913 adaptation of the ancient Greek myth of Pygmalion. Pygmalion, a sculptor and king, creates a statue of an idealized woman. He falls in love with his ideal and prays to Venus to bring the statue to life. Venus grants his request. Professor Higgins (Rex Harrison) is the early 1900s version of Pygmalion.

Something you might remember... Rex Harrison and Julie Andrews starred in the stage version. It was expected that Andrews would reprise her role for the film. Walt Disney even offered to delay the filming of *Mary Poppins* for Andrews' sake. But Jack Warner chose Audrey Hepburn (pictured) to play Eliza Doolittle.

Something new to remember... In 1995, the Barbie Hollywood Legends Collection issued Eliza Doolittle and Henry Higgins dolls.

1964

First broadcast of *Gilligan's Island*

Just sit right back and you'll hear a tale
A tale of a fateful trip
That started from this tropic port
Aboard this tiny ship

The mate was a mighty sailin' man
The skipper brave and sure
Five passengers set sail that day
For a three-hour tour, a three-hour tour...

Created by Sherwood Schwartz, the show featured Bob Denver (pictured), Alan Hale, Jim Backus, Natalie Schafer, Tina Louise, Russell Johnson, and Dawn Wells.

Something you might remember... During the first season's opening song, the harbor's American flag is at half-mast because filming took place just after President John F. Kennedy's assassination.

Something new to remember... The *SS Minnow* was sarcastically named for Federal Communications Commission chief Newton Minow, who labeled television a "vast wasteland."

THE DINOSAURS	NOTABLE WOMEN	OXFORD ENGLISH DICTIONARY	NAME THAT INSTRUMENT	BELGIUM	COMPOSERS BY COUNTRY
$200	$200	$200	$200	$200	$200
$400	$400	$400	$400	$400	$400
$600	$600	$600	$600	$600	$600
$800	$800	$800	$800	$800	$800
$1000	$1000	$1000	$1000	$1000	$1000

1964

First broadcast of *Jeopardy!*

Created by game show mogul Merv Griffin and hosted by Art Fleming, the show ran in a daytime slot from 1964 until 1974. A weekly nighttime show was tried next, but didn't fare well. *The All-New Jeopardy!* ran briefly during the daytime, from October 1978 until March 1979. But on September 10, 1984, *Jeopardy!* returned with new host Alex Trebek. Since then, it has become one of the most popular game shows ever, winning a record number of Emmys and adapted for international use.

Something you might remember... Griffin credits his wife with the idea for the show. He originally titled it, *What's the Question*, but shelved the name when a network exec told him that the working concept of the show "doesn't have enough jeopardies."

Something new to remember...*Jeopardy!* isn't the first TV game show to use an answer-and-question format. The first to do so was the *CBS Television Quiz* hosted by Gil Fates, which aired from July 1941 until May 1942.

1965

The Supremes release "Stop! In the Name of Love"

Written by Motown's prolific writing team of Holland–Dozier–Holland, the song rapidly topped the *Billboard* Hot 100. The Supremes had a dozen number one hits between 1964 and 1969, second only to the Beatles. Both black and white audiences loved the group, paving the way for other crossover artists like the Temptations and the Jackson 5. As one of Ed Sullivan's favorite groups, the Supremes appeared on his show sixteen times.

Something you might remember... The famous one-hand on the hip and the other outstretched in a stop gesture move was choreographed by Paul Williams and Melvin Franklin of the Temptations, who taught the group the move backstage, just before they appeared on a London TV special.

Something new to remember... The Jackson 5 covered the song on *The Carol Burnett Show* in 1975.

1965

The Sound of Music premieres

The film is based on the Rogers and Hammerstein Broadway musical by the same name. Both are based on the book *The Story of the Trapp Family Singers* by the (real) Maria von Trapp. Songs such as "Do-Re-Mi," "Edelweiss," "Climb Ev'ry Mountain," and "Sixteen Going on Seventeen" are timeless. Julie Andrews (pictured) loved her role as Maria. It was a very successful follow-up to her starring role in *Mary Poppins.*

Something you might remember..."Edelweiss" is not a traditional Austrian folk song nor is it the Austrian national anthem. It was written by Rodgers and Hammerstein for Captain von Trapp to sing.

Something new to remember... Who referred to the movie as the "Sound of Mucus?" Christopher Plummer (Captain von Trapp). He didn't like making the film and has said that working with Julie Andrews (the two are friends) was like "being hit over the head with a big Valentine's Day card, every day."

1965

First broadcast of *Get Smart*

Creators Mel Brooks and Buck Henry combined James Bond with Inspector Clouseau (both very popular at the time) to create Maxwell Smart (Don Adams). He was joined by Agent 99 (Barbara Feldon). In an October 1965 *Time* magazine article, Brooks said, "I was sick of looking at all those nice sensible situation comedies. They were such distortions of life. If a maid ever took over my house like Hazel, I'd set her hair on fire. I wanted to do a crazy, unreal comic-strip kind of thing about something besides a family."

Something you might remember...The show featured hilarious secret gizmos like the Cone of Silence (which often malfunctions), the shoe phone, and the contents of the shoe, which could include explosive pellets, smoke bombs, or a suicide pill (which Max believes is for the enemy).

Something new to remember...*Get Smart* is the only Mel Brooks creation with a laugh track. Was it really even necessary?

1965

First broadcast of *I Dream of Jeannie*

OK, so maybe the show wasn't a high point in American TV, but it is stuck in our collective memory. *I Dream of Jeannie*, (sounds a lot like "genie") was NBC's answer to *Bewitched*. Creator Sidney Sheldon was reportedly inspired by the film *The Brass Bottle*, starring Tony Randall, Barbara Eden, and Burl Ives (as the genie). At first, Sheldon insisted that a brunette play Jeannie, since a blonde would be too similar to Elizabeth Montgomery. But he just couldn't find the right brunette and ended up signing Eden (pictured).

Something you might remember...Larry Hagman (pictured) played Jeannie's Master, Major Anthony Nelson. And Bill Daily played Major Roger Healey. Hagman went on to *Dallas,* and Daily later played Bob Newhart's neighbor across the hall.

Something new to remember...Jeannie's bottle prop was actually an empty Jim Beam bourbon whiskey decanter. There's no indication who drank the bottle dry.

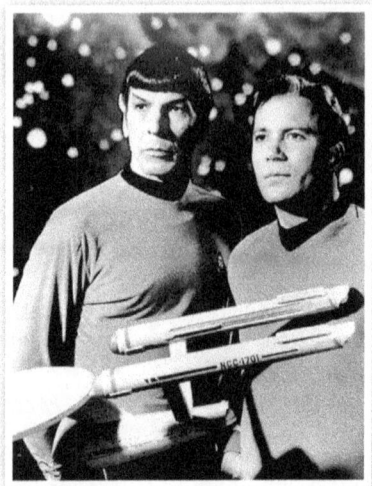

1966

First broadcast of *Star Trek*

Captain's Log. Star date 1966...
Though originally broadcast for only three seasons on NBC, the original Star Trek series has spawned six TV series and a dozen films. Original series stars included William Shatner (Captain James T. Kirk), Leonard Nimoy (Science Officer Spock), DeForest Kelley (Dr. Leonard "Bones" McCoy), James Doohan (Montgomery "Scotty" Scott), and Nichelle Nichols (Communications Officer Nyota Uhura).

Something you might remember... The crew's uniforms are color-coded. Gold shirts are the command uniforms; red is for operations, and blue is for the sciences and medicine.

Something new to remember... In two episodes, the show borrowed the *Andy Griffith* Mayberry town set. Characters walk by the courthouse and Floyd's barbershop.

1966

First broadcast of *Batman*

Batman, starring Adam West, Burt Ward, and Yvonne Craig as Batgirl, was on for three seasons. For the first two seasons, the show was broadcast twice a week, with an announcer ending the first night's cliff-hanger by intoning, "Tune in tomorrow—same Bat-time, same Bat-channel!"

Something you might remember... Guest villains included Frank Gorshin (the Riddler), Burgess Meredith (the Penguin), Cesar Romero (the Joker), and Julie Newmar/Eartha Kitt (Catwoman). "Batclimb" cameos, with guest actors popping out of windows for a conversation, featured Werner Klemperer as Col. Klink, Dick Clark, Sammy Davis Jr., Art Linkletter, and many others.

Something new to remember... The Penguin was so popular that reportedly the show's producers kept a script ready and any time Burgess Meredith was in Los Angeles, he was welcome to do an episode.

1967

Aretha Franklin releases "Respect"

Those who were at the recording of "Respect" and witnessed Aretha playing the piano and belting out her vocals knew that this song was going to be something special. In many ways, it was the beginning of her reign as the Queen of Soul. "Respect" quickly reached number one on multiple charts. The song became a rallying cry for both the civil rights and feminist movements. It remains Franklin's signature song.

Something you might remember... Otis Redding (often called the King of Soul) actually wrote the song and included it on his album, *Otis Blue,* in 1965. But while the lyrics of Redding's version demanded respect from his woman, Franklin's version demanded respect from her man.

Something new to remember... In 1987, Franklin was the first woman inducted into the Rock and Roll Hall of Fame. She has sold more than seventy-five million records, won eighteen Grammy Awards, and had more than forty Top 40 singles.

1967

Sidney Poitier stars in *Guess Who's Coming to Dinner?*

Sidney Poitier, Harry Belafonte, and Charlton Heston at the Civil Rights March on Washington, 1963.

This groundbreaking film about an interracial romantic relationship stars Sidney Poitier, Katharine Hepburn, Spencer Tracy, and Katharine Houghton. Tracy was gravely ill during production and died just days after filming wrapped up.

Something you might remember... The movie played in theaters throughout 1968. It contains the following exchange between Joey (the white daughter) and Tillie (the black maid). Joey asks, "Guess who's coming to dinner now?" Tillie sarcastically replies, "The Reverend Martin Luther King?" After King's assassination on April 4, 1968, the line was removed from theater copies for a time.

Something new to remember... In 2005, the film *Guess Who* was released starring Bernie Mac and Ashton Kutcher. A comedy, the roles are reversed (the girlfriend's family is black and the boyfriend is white).

1968

First broadcast of
Mr. Rogers' Neighborhood

Concerned about the quality of children's programming, Fred McFeely Rogers created a program for children that would nourish the mind, body, and spirit of each one of his viewers. His vision resulted in *Mr. Rogers' Neighborhood.* Rogers was a gentle man who emanated unconditional love and encouragement. For decades, he was a reassuring father figure to many children.

Something you might remember... There are so many characters in the "real" neighborhood and the Neighborhood of Make Believe, including Chef Brockett, Officer Clemmons, Mr. McFeely (Speedy Delivery!), Guitarist Joe Negri/Handyman Negri, King Friday XIII, Queen Sara Saturday, X The Owl, Henrietta Pussycat, Daniel Striped Tiger, Dr. Duckbill Platypus, Lady Aberlin, and, of course, Lady Elaine Fairchilde and her spinning museum!

Something new to remember... Mr. Rogers was an inspiration to both parents and children. He said, "Parents are like shuttles on a loom. They join the threads of the past with threads of the future and leave their own bright patterns as they go."

1968

Marvin Gaye releases "I Heard It Through the Grapevine"

Smokey Robinson & The Miracles recorded the song first, but their version was rejected by Motown owner Barry Gordy because he didn't feel it was hit material. In 1967, Marvin Gaye (pictured) recorded the song, but Gordy rejected it too. Finally, Gladys Knight & The Pips received Gordy's blessing to release their version, which topped the charts. Meanwhile, Gaye's version was put on his 1968 album, *In the Groove*. DJs began playing it and when Gordy finally agreed to release Gaye's version as a single, the song shot up to the top of the *Billboard* Pop Singles chart, remaining there for seven weeks.

Something you might remember... The California Raisins covered the song in the eighties.

Something new to remember... Barrett Strong, the singer on "Money (That's What I Want)," came up with the song's concept while visiting Michigan Avenue in Chicago where he frequently heard the phrase, "I heard it through the grapevine."

1968

First broadcast of *Rowan & Martin's Laugh-In*

There were one hundred forty subversive, witty, and hip episodes of *Laugh-In*, beginning in January 1968 and ending in March 1973. Hosts Dan Rowan and Dick Martin (both pictured) welcomed regulars such as Ruth Buzzi, Goldie Hawn, Arte Johnson, Jo Anne Worley, and Lilly Tomlin. Regular guests included: Jack Benny, Johnny Carson, Sammy Davis Jr., Zsa Zsa Gabor, Tiny Tim, and Flip Wilson.

Something you might remember... During the 1968 presidential campaign, both Richard Nixon and Hubert Humphrey were invited to make cameo appearances. While Humphrey declined, Nixon accepted and deadpanned, "Sock it to me?" Ironically, *Laugh-In* may have helped Richard Nixon get elected.

Something new to remember... The show's "News of the Future" segment actually predicted the presidency of then-California Governor Ronald Reagan, as well as the fall of the Berlin Wall in 1989. As Edith Ann would say, "And that's the truth. Thppp."

1969

Woodstock

About half a million hippies came to Woodstock, held on Max Yasgur's dairy farm near Bethel, New York. Prior to the festival, locals voiced their opposition to Woodstock, including a large sign that read, "Buy No Milk. Stop Max's Hippy Music Festival."

Something you might remember... Artists appearing included Santana; the Grateful Dead; Janis Joplin; Sly & The Family Stone; The Who; Jefferson Airplane; Crosby, Stills, Nash & Young; and Jimi Hendrix.

Something new to remember... John Fogarty recalled Creedence Clearwater Revival's 3:30 a.m. start time: "We waited and waited and finally it was our turn...There were a half million people asleep. These people were out...all intertwined and asleep, covered with mud. And this is the moment I will never forget...a quarter mile away in the darkness...there was some guy flicking his Bic, and in the night I hear, 'Don't worry about it John. We're with you.' I played the rest of the show for that guy."

1969

First broadcast of *Sesame Street*

Sesame Street tries to use the "addictive qualities of television and do something good with them." The show was the first preschool program to use educational and developmental research in its design. Executive Director Joan Ganz Cooney brought together a team of former *Captain Kangaroo* production people for the show. Jim Henson and his Muppets were added to the mix, turning the Muppets into stars.

Something you might remember...Ernie singing "Rubber Duckie"...Big Bird's teddy bear, "Radar," named after Radar from *M*A*S*H*...Ernie's sweater has horizontal stripes to make him appear relaxed; Bert wears vertical stripes to appear uptight.

Something new to remember...The show was sued for the song "Letter B" (a parody of the Beatles' "Let It Be"). The Beatles no longer owned the rights to the song, and even wrote an affidavit supporting *Sesame Street*. The case was settled for just $500.

1969

First broadcast of *The Brady Bunch*

For five seasons, America watched Greg, Marcia, Peter, Jan, Bobby, and Cindy experience the joys and trials of growing up. While most episodes were written from the standpoint of the children, Florence Henderson (Carol Brady), Robert Reed (Mike Brady), and Ann B. Davis (Alice) are active and involved adults, making it a show that can be enjoyed by viewers of all ages.

Something you might remember... Producer Sherwood Schwartz cowrote the opening song. Like *Gilligan's Island,* Schwartz laid out the show's premise in the theme song, rather than dealing with it in the story itself.

Something new to remember... Though the Brady bathroom was often seen, due to network censors not once did viewers see a toilet. The joke at the time was that the Bradys were so wholesome, they didn't even go to the bathroom.

1969

First broadcast of *Hee Haw*

Inspired by *Laugh-In* and hosted by Buck Owens and Roy Clark, *Hee Haw* first aired in the summer of 1969 on CBS, replacing *The Smothers Brothers Comedy Hour.* After a few seasons on CBS, it ran for over twenty years in first-run syndication. The show was popular with country folk and city slickers, and had success in all of its major markets, including New York, Los Angeles, and Chicago.

Something you might remember... Popular skits and features included, "PFFT! You Was Gone!;" "The Haystack;" "Pickin' and Grinnin';" "Junior Samples' used car sales;" "Gloom, Despair and Agony On Me;" "Hee Haw Salutes;" "The Cornfield Jokes;" and the "Hee Haw Gospel Quartet."

Something new to remember... The series was shot in "blocks." The whole cast would gather for a week in June and again in October and shoot all the skits and scenes. Individual shows were edited together later. Roy Clark compared the weeklong gatherings to "a big family reunion."

1971

Soul Train, hosted by Don Cornelius, goes national

In the late 1960s, *Soul Train* creator and host Don Cornelius (second from right in photo) was a news analyst and sports reporter at Chicago TV station WCIU, while also hosting "record hops" at area high schools. He referred to his traveling dance parties as "The Soul Train." In 1970, WCIU brought *Soul Train* to TV. The show went national in 1971 and the train kept on rolling for thirty-five years. It featured R&B, soul and hip hop artists, with a smattering of funk, disco, and gospel. Guests included Michael Jackson, Paula Abdul, James Brown, David Bowie, Ike and Tina Turner, Parliament-Funkadelic, and the 5th Dimension.

Something you might remember... Who can forget the "Soul Train Line?"

Something new to remember... Cornelius admittedly struggled with hip hop. He felt it didn't reflect positively on African American culture (one of the show's primary goals).

1971

First broadcast of *All in the Family*

Norman Lear's *All in the Family* and its spinoffs, including *Maude* and *The Jeffersons*, dominated TV in the 1970s. Carroll O'Connor (Archie), Jean Stapleton (Edith), Sally Struthers (Gloria), and Rob Reiner (Michael, a.k.a. "Meathead") were guests in our homes for almost the entire decade. Using humor, the show illustrated the absurdity of bigotry. Viewers loved it, making it the first TV show to top ratings for five consecutive seasons.

Something you might remember... This was the first prime-time TV show to feature the sound of a toilet flushing.

Something new to remember... When Jean Stapleton grew tired of playing Edith (as part of the spin-off, *Archie Bunker's Place*), Norman Lear reportedly struggled with how to tastefully have Edith die. Stapleton reminded Lear, "She's only fiction." After a pause, Lear responded, "To me, she isn't only fiction."

1971

Don McLean releases "American Pie"

Don McLean's magnum opus to Buddy Holly and his cryptic commentary on a chaotic America is also one of the greatest feel-good songs. But what does the eight-minute-and-thirty-six-second-long song mean? When asked about its meaning, McLean has maintained what he calls a "dignified silence," though he has jokingly said, "It means I don't ever have to work again if I don't want to." Of course, that hasn't stopped others from guessing. Some believe, for instance, that the Jester is Bob Dylan and Satan could be Mick Jagger.

Something you might remember... McLean has admitted that the song is more than just about Buddy Holly: "Only the beginning is about Buddy Holly, and the rest of it goes on and talks about America and politics and the country...especially in 1970 and '71, when it was very turbulent."

Something new to remember... The first group to cover the song was, unfortunately, the Brady Bunch. It was on their 1972 album, *Meet the Brady Bunch*. Even Greg (Barry Williams) admits it was horrible.

1972

First broadcast of *M*A*S*H*

For eleven seasons, M*A*S*H (Mobile Army Surgical Hospital) was America's running commentary on war and peace. Characters included Captain Pierce, a.k.a. "Hawkeye" (Alan Alda); Major Margaret Houlihan, a.k.a. "Hot Lips" (Loretta Swit); Corporal Max Klinger (Jamie Farr); Father Francis Mulcahy (William Christopher); Colonel Sherman T. Potter (Harry Morgan); Captain B.J. Hunnicut (Mike Farrell); Corporal O'Reilly, a.k.a. "Radar" (Gary Burghoff); Major Charles Winchester (David Ogden Stiers); Major Frank Burns (Larry Linville); Captain John McIntyre, a.k.a. "Trapper" (Wayne Rogers); and Lt. Colonel Henry Blake (McLean Stevenson).

Something you might remember... The show's producers objected to a laugh track. The compromise was a "chuckle track" used sparingly, but never during scenes in surgery.

Something new to remember... Gary Burghoff played Charlie Brown in the 1967 musical, *You're a Good Man, Charlie Brown.*

1972

First broadcast of *The (New) Price is Right*

Created by Mark Goodson and Bill Todman, the original version of the show ran from 1956 to 1965. The *New Price Is Right* premiered on September 4, 1972, with host Bob Barker (pictured). As the show caught on, the "new" was dropped. Now, over forty years and 7,500 episodes later, over $250 million in prizes has been given away.

Something you might remember... When a contestant spins the Big Wheel, it has to go all the way around or the audience boos and another spin is required. Once, Bob Barker himself spun the Big Wheel for a contestant in a wheelchair—but the wheel didn't go all the way around. Barker was booed, of course, and he quipped that this was "the most humiliating moment of my life."

Something new to remember..."Vanna White! Come on down!" In 1980, a pre-*Wheel of Fortune* Vanna was a contestant on *The Price Is Right*. At one point, Barker scolds her for watching herself on the TV monitor.

1972

The Godfather premieres

Marlon Brando at the Civil Rights March on Washington, 1963.

In 2007, *The Godfather* was ranked by the American Film Institute as one of the greatest films, second only to *Citizen Kane*. Family patriarch Vito Corleone (Marlon Brando) transforms Michael Corleone (Al Pacino) from innocent family member to bloody Mafia boss.

Something you might remember... Don Vito Corleone says, "I'm gonna make him an offer he can't refuse."

Something new to remember... Real gangsters liked the film. "Sammy the Bull" Gravano, the former Gamino crime family underboss, said, "I left that movie stunned. I mean I floated out of the theater...That was our life. It was incredible. I remember talking to a multitude of guys...who felt exactly the same way." The movie even influenced the Mafia culture. Reportedly, Patriarca crime family member Paulie Intiso changed the way he spoke, imitating Vito Corleone. Intiso swore frequently and used poor grammar, but after seeing the movie, he became more articulate and philosophical.

1973

Jesus Christ Superstar premieres

One of the most controversial, powerful, and inspirational films of the 1970s, *Jesus Christ Superstar* is based on the rock opera of the same name by Andrew Lloyd Webber and Tim Rice. For some, the film was controversial because it embellished the gospel accounts, delving into the psychology and relationships of Jesus (Ted Neeley, pictured), Judas, and Mary Magdalene. But its purpose was to tell a story and relate that story in a contemporary way—something the Gospels themselves do.

Something you might remember... The final scene showing the empty cross also features, accidentally, a shepherd and sheep walking across the frame. The scene was used in the film because it was a stunning visual symbol of the resurrection of the Good Shepherd.

Something new to remember... Mickey Dolenz (the Monkees), David Cassidy (the Partridge Family), and John Travolta were also considered for the role of Christ.

1974

First Broadcast of *Happy Days*

There was a time when Fonzie (Henry Winkler) was cool—*really* cool. Especially when compared to Richie Cunningham (Ron Howard). *Happy Days* was originally just a segment on *Love, American Style*. But with the success of the movie, *American Graffiti* (also starring Ron Howard), ABC became interested in *Happy Days* as a series. Fred Silverman, head of CBS programming, tried to stop the show's rising popularity by scheduling *Good Times* directly opposite the show. It worked, but when Silverman moved over to ABC in 1975, he restored *Happy Days* to the top of the ratings.

Something you might remember... Many think that the show's quality began to deteriorate after season five began with Fonzie jumping a shark while water-skiing in his leather jacket. The phrase "jumping the shark" came to refer to a TV show that begins to drop in quality.

Something new to remember... Fonzie carries a Lone Ranger photo in his wallet.

1975

Jaws premieres

It was one of Steven Spielberg's first films, and production was 104 days behind schedule, doubling the cost of making the film. Spielberg figured his career as a director was over. But when *Jaws* became the first summer blockbuster movie, all was forgiven.

Something you might remember... During filming, the three full-size pneumatically powered sharks, nicknamed "Bruce," were constantly malfunctioning and often were not available. Spielberg had to adapt by hinting that the shark was near or using the camera as the shark's eyes. Those changes improved the film, giving it the suspense of an Alfred Hitchcock thriller.

Something new to remember... Filming had gone so badly that Spielberg feared the crew would throw him into the water once production was completed. On the last day of shooting, just before filming the final scene (the exploding shark), Spielberg jumped into a speedboat and sped toward the shore, yelling, "I shall not return!"

1977

Roots miniseries airs

The miniseries was based on Alex Haley's novel, *Roots: The Saga of an American Family.* It was the first time Americans had seen such extensive African American history. ABC was worried the series would be a ratings disaster, so the network aired it on eight consecutive nights, hoping to get it out of the way. But it wasn't a ratings disaster. In fact, it was so popular that the final episode was the third-highest rated TV program ever.

Something you might remember... Actors included LeVar Burton as young Kunta Kinte; John Amos as older Kunta Kinte; Olivia Cole as Mathilda; Louis Gossett Jr. as Fiddler; Ben Vereen as "Chicken" George Moore; Edward Asner as Captain Davies; Robert Reed as Dr. William Reynolds; Cicely Tyson as Binta; and Maya Angelou as Nyo Boto.

Something new to remember...*Roots* won nine Emmy awards. It remains the most popular miniseries in US history.

1977

Star Wars premieres

It's hard to overestimate the impact of *Star Wars* on audiences. Today's computer graphics are taken for granted, but in 1977, the special effects in this film were amazing. The soundtrack was composed and conducted by John Williams. His stunning score was ranked the number one film score of all time by the American Film Institute. These and many other elements made *Star Wars* the top grossing film up to that point, earning almost $800 million at the box office.

Something you might remember... Characters we all know include Darth Vader (voiced by James Earl Jones), Han Solo (Harrison Ford), Luke Skywalker (Mark Hamill's film debut), Princess Leia (Carrie Fisher), C-3PO, R2-D2, Obi-Wan "Ben" Kenobi (Alec Guinness), Chewbacca, and the ever-present Force.

Something new to remember... Desert scenes were filmed in Tunisia. At one point, the Libyan government reportedly threatened to mobilize its military because the Jawa sandcrawler was too close to its border and the Libyans feared it was a military vehicle.

1977

Saturday Night Fever premieres

John Belushi parodied the film in "Samurai Night Fever" on *Saturday Night Live.* In *Airplane!* Robert Hays imitated John Travolta's disco pose (and so have millions of us). Even Rudy Giuliani reportedly revealed his inner Travolta by dancing to "Disco Inferno" at a celebrity event. It was this movie that ignited the disco craze. The soundtrack, featuring the Bee Gees (Barry, Robin, and Maurice Gibb), is one of the best-selling soundtracks.

Something you might remember... Many people enjoyed disco dancing to "Stayin' Alive," "How Deep Is Your Love," "Night Fever," "More Than a Woman," "If I Can't Have You," and "You Should Be Dancing."

Something new to remember... The movie was film critic Gene Siskel's favorite. He said that "Travolta on the dance floor is like a peacock on amphetamines. He struts like crazy." Siskel even bought Travolta's white polyester disco suit at a charity auction.

1978

First broadcast of *Dallas*

The OPEC oil crises of the 1970s caused the price of gasoline to soar. Overnight, oil companies became villains. Enter J.R. Ewing and Ewing Oil. Millions of Americans watched with fascination the machinations of these powerful fictional Texas oil barons. For fourteen years, viewers loved to hate J.R.

Something you might remember... The soap opera's characters include J.R. Ewing (Larry Hagman), Jock Ewing (Jim Davis), Cliff Barnes (Ken Kercheval), Bobby Ewing (Patrick Duffy), Sue Ellen Ewing (Linda Gray), Miss Ellie Ewing (Barbara Bel Geddes), Pamela Barnes Ewing (Victoria Principal), Clayton Farlow (Howard Keel), and Lucy Ewing Cooper (Charlene Tilton).

Something new to remember...*Dallas* was popular in Communist Romania. The government aired it because they thought the show was anti-capitalist. But the Romanian people saw a whole new world and wanted the same for themselves. A few years after the communists were ousted, Larry Hagman visited Romania—as a hero.

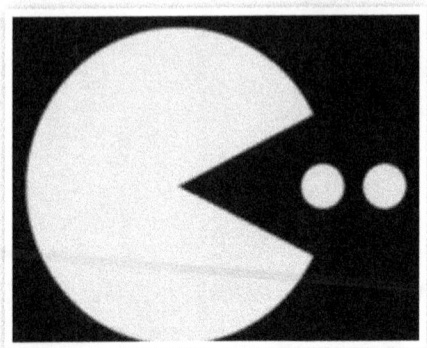

1980

The *Pac-Man* video game is released

Developed in Japan, *Pac-Man* made its debut during the "golden age of arcade video games," when the new games were rapidly replacing pinball machines. Video arcades sprung up across America. In those dark dens, with flashing lights and strange noises, there were already classics such as *Space Invaders* and *Asteroids*. But *Pac-Man* blew them all away. It quickly grossed over $1 billion—a quarter at a time—even surpassing the revenues of *Star Wars*.

Something you might remember... The goblins that chase *Pac-Man* seem to move randomly, but their movements are actually programmed. Advanced players have learned to use this to their advantage.

Something new to remember... Although the game was designed to never end, a bug in the program means that the game ends at level 256. At that level, the program creates random symbols over the entire right half of the screen, making it impossible to go on.

1980

The Rubik's Cube begins selling in America

The Rubik's Cube was invented in 1974 by Hungarian professor Erno Rubik, who was simply interested in solving the structural design problem of moving the blocks independently without the cube falling apart. Once he designed the cube, he tested it by rotating and mixing the colors. When he tried to restore his cube, he realized he had invented a puzzle (with 43 quintillion combinations). The cube was introduced to America on May 5, 1980, at a party hosted by Hungarian actress and socialite Zsa Zsa Gabor. Since its invention, over 350 million cubes have been sold around the world.

Something you might remember... What is the fewest number of moves needed to solve the cube? In 2010, researchers used computer time donated by Google to prove the so-called "God's Number" to be twenty.

Something new to remember... The speed record for solving the cube is 5.55 seconds for two hands, 9.05 seconds for one hand, and 23.80 seconds for solving it blindfolded.

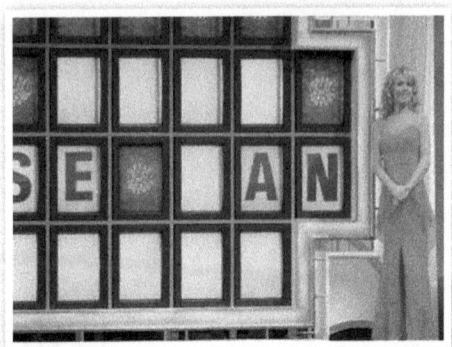

1983

First nighttime broadcast of *Wheel of Fortune*

Although Merv Griffin had already created a daytime version of the program, it wasn't until the nighttime show began that "America's Game" started its meteoric rise in popularity. The show has been ranked by *TV Guide* as second only to *Jeopardy!* The enduring combination of Pat Sajak and Vanna White has kept the show popular for over thirty years.

Something you might remember...*Guinness World Records* has recognized Vanna White as the "Most Frequent Clapper." She claps over one hundred thousand times each season and has clapped about 3.5 million times since 1983.

Something new to remember... The show has been parodied on *Sesame Street*. A Muppet named Pat Playjacks hosts "Squeal of Fortune." Contestants Prairie Dawn and the Count spin the wheel and guess how many times a pig in the center of the wheel will squeal before the wheel stops. Of course, the Count wins.

1983

Michael Jackson releases his *Thriller* video

MTV was only two years old when *Thriller* premiered on the network. The thirteen-minute video took just four days to shoot, but cost an unprecedented $500,000 to produce (music video budgets at the time averaged $50,000). Over 9 million copies of the video have been sold. But the impact of the video goes beyond the numbers. The incredible music and dancing made this one of the most important artistic efforts of the 1980s.

Something you might remember... Because Jackson was a Jehovah's Witness, he placed this disclaimer at the beginning of the film: "Due to my strong personal convictions, I wish to stress that this film in no way endorses a belief in the occult."

Something new to remember... According to the designer of Jackson's red jacket worn in the video, Jackson weighed only ninety-nine pounds and had a 26-inch waist—exactly the same measurements as Fred Astaire.

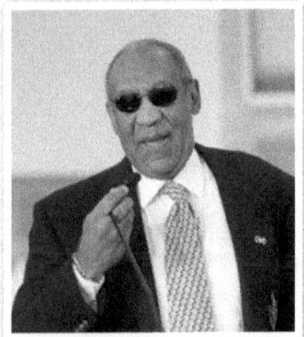

1984

First broadcast of *The Cosby Show*

*T*V *Guide* has ranked Cliff Huxtable as TV's greatest dad. It's really no surprise. For eight seasons, the Huxtables came into our homes each Thursday night, portraying a successful and educated family. It was the biggest TV hit of the 1980s (number one in the Nielsen ratings for five consecutive seasons—only *All in the Family* and *American Idol* share this record).

Something you might remember... Other stars included Phylicia Rashad as Clair Hanks Huxtable, Lisa Bonet as Denise, Malcolm-Jamal Warner as Theodore (Theo), Tempestt Bledsoe as Vanessa, Keshia Knight Pulliam as Rudy, and Sabrina Le Beauf as Sondra.

Something new to remember... The show began airing on NBC opposite the very popular *Magnum, P.I.* and was not expected to do well. But it quickly became the number-one show and usually beat *Magnum* in the ratings. In one episode, Bill Cosby (pictured) wore a *Magnum* baseball cap, as a hat-tip to his friend Tom Selleck.